101
REINING TIPS

Also by Laren Sellers

Training and Showing the Versatility Ranch Horse

101 Basics of Training and Showing
REINING TIPS

Laren Sellers

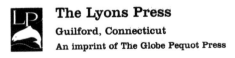

The Lyons Press
Guilford, Connecticut
An imprint of The Globe Pequot Press

The Lyons Press is an imprint of The Globe Pequot Press.

10 9 8 7 6 5 4 3 2 1

Printed in the United States of America

ISBN-13: 978-1-59228-860-1
ISBN-10: 1-59228-860-X

Library of Congress Cataloging-in-Publication Data is available on file.

Dedication

This book is dedicated to Drew.

Words are insufficient to accurately describe the joy and love you've added to my life. Thank you for having faith in me.

Contents

Introduction

According to the National Reining Horse Association, reining is a judged event designed to show the athletic ability of a ranch type horse within the confines of a show arena. In NRHA competition, contestants are required to run one of ten approved patterns, included in the NRHA Handbook.

Each pattern includes small slow circles, large fast circles, flying lead changes, roll-backs over the hocks, 360 degree spins done in place, and exciting sliding stops that are the hallmark of the reining horse.

My first experience on a true reining horse took place in Bow, Washington, with AQHA trainer Sue Sultze. It lasted only a few hours and we only practiced a few of the simple maneuvers, but I knew immediately that I was riding a horse that possessed far more talent and ability than I could properly control.

That brief time in the saddle gave me a respect for the intricate knowledge that comes with showing a reining horse. Doing research for this book only validated that original idea. The sport has been associated with the beauty and concise moves that one might see in figure skating. Powerful. Beautiful. Memorable. The horse-handling expertise required to achieve that beautiful movement takes years of dedicated practice.

Reining horses command advanced training to produce response from the slightest cues of the rider. When that teamwork comes together the display of speed-controlled circles and spectacular sliding stops can render a person speechless.

In the United States, the major associations hosting reining competitions are the National Reining Horse Association and the American Quarter Horse Association. The United States Equestrian Foundation governs the sport nationally while the Fédération Equestre Internationale (FEI) governs international competitions.

The basic principles of reining competition are universal. Reining captivates horse enthusiasts with artistic and crowd appeal. The worldwide popularity of the sport has currently pushed reining to the threshold of being an Olympic event. The last time an equestrian event was tacked onto the Olympics was in 1912. In 2002, reining was added as the seventh event to be featured at the World Equestrian Games. As the sport of reining draws more and more attention from the FEI, the worldwide playing field for reining enthusiasts is growing every day.

Chapter 1

Let's Get Started

Begin your reining education with the basics. Creating a strong foundation by knowing the rules, attending a competition, and creating a relationship with a reining mentor will establish solid ground for your reining adventure.

tip 1. Play by the rules

Want to compete in various reining associations? The first thing to do isn't finding the date of the next show: it's finding a rulebook, then reading it. While many associations base their rules on the National Reining Horse Association rulebook, each can have its own spin on, for example, the spin maneuver.

It is invaluable to read not only what the patterns require but also how the judges will be examining each part for faults. If you are aware that you dropped gait in a large circle, then being docked for it in your score will be the logical reprimand.

If you want to play, remember to play by the rules. The rules will impact every part of your tack, from bits to bell boots, and can even dictate the exact type of horseshoes your mount should be wearing. Read the rules prior to signing up for a competition, prior to training your horse, and even prior to buying your horse. Some breeds can perform better than others in this sport.

tip 2. Green and green clash

Horses that have just begun training, say sixty rides, are considered *greenbroke*. Similarly, a person fresh on the show scene is also considered *green*. The saying "Green and green do not match" is a reminder that a person who is new to the horse industry is discouraged from purchasing a horse that is also green. It is best if one of the two can help to educate the other.

If you are an inexperienced reining enthusiast, find a horse that knows the ropes. An older show horse is often the perfect teacher. If you are an experienced horse person (i.e., this means having much more exposure to horses than recreational trail riding or spending a weekend at a dude ranch), you can gauge what level of training you can deal with in your horse. But be ready for a greenbroke horse to require loads of patience, dedication, and slow progress.

In the event of reining, a bad combination of horse and rider can create quick disillusionment with the sport and some bad habits in the horse. Select your mount carefully before proceeding.

As a spectator, you'll have the opportunity to see fabulous sliding stops like the one in this photo. (photo courtesy of AQHA)

tip 3. Be a spectator

Once you've read the rulebook and studied your topic, get to a show. But leave your horse at home. You need to sit in the stands and watch a competition. Keeping track of the horses you thought performed well in each class and comparing that data to the judges' placings can help you learn about the sport.

Reining is a thrilling spectator sport with flashy moves and thoroughly trained horses. With speed and agility the horses will complete the prescribed patterns with almost no visual cues from their riders. During this time, notice how the pattern that might have looked confusing in the rulebook is played out in the arena.

A show is full of people who love to talk about their horses. Take the time to visit with exhibitors and other spectators. In little time you will hear specific bloodlines repeated again and again. This can lead you toward a strong pedigree when you look to purchase your horse.

Requesting assistance from a professional trainer can improve your horseback experiences.

tip 4. Seek professional help

At one point or another, many of us have toyed with the idea of seeking professional help—and some horse enthusiasts who haven't yet thought of it should. When it comes to working with high-dollar horses needing to perform precise movements, the professional horse trainer can be necessary. When searching for a professional, remember that you are paying for their service—meaning if you don't have faith in their talent to get you and your horse to show to your potential, fire the professional. It can take several attempts to find the best trainer to work with you and your horse. Treat this like a business transaction. If it isn't working for the business, end the partnership. Utilize the Web sites of the top reining associations for lists of professional trainers in your areas, if you are Internet savvy.

A good reining mentor will take the time to explain answers to your questions.

tip 5. Find a reining mentor

Due to the solo nature of reining, it is a sport that requires an ability to allow your own mistakes to happen—yet still get back out there to compete again. To help you adjust to this commanding type of performance, find a mentor with the same approach to showing as you have, but someone with more showing experience. A good place to look? The barn where you keep your horse or your trainer's barn. Or just start up a conversation with someone whose showing style you admire at your next event.

A mentor can help you adjust to the stresses of showing. And as much as you might think you are the only person who has ever flubbed a stop or blown a pattern, truth is, it has all been done before. Let your mentor relay their experiences with specific shows, horses, trainers, etc. and examine that information to see how it applies to your shows. Let them be your guide to what can be accomplished in your region with your reining horse and where you can strive to take your horse next show season.

tip 6. In the blood

Check out the bloodlines of any horse before you make a purchase. Looking at how the horse was bred can help you decide if there is the likelihood that reining will complement the bloodlines of the horse. It is important to look at both the top and bottom sides of the breeding and compare these lines with horses you know of as good reiners. Horses with generation after generation of breeding for reining competition will generally outperform horses not bred for this sport.

Refer to the National Reining Horse Association Web site (www.nrha.com) for a quick look at million dollar sires and hall-of-famers. Also, *The American Quarter Horse Journal* designates the October issue as their Reining and Reined Cow Horse Issue. Inside, you'll find multiple breakdowns of NRHA and AQHA point leaders and money earners of sires and dams.

tip 7. Get educated, creatively

Break out the library card and read up on reining, horse breeds, anything and everything that might help you succeed in this sport. Join the American Quarter Horse Association and the National Reining Horse Association, or at least find out what it would take to be in those groups and compete in their events. Check out television shows like those on RFD-TV* to learn more about reining. Attend clinics in your area on judging reining classes to understand what you'll be scored on once you enter the show ring. Once you feel like you understand the ins and outs of the sport, it's time to get the gear (saddle and horse, to name a few) into your hot little hands!

* RFD-TV is a twenty-four hour television network that features topics aimed at the interests of rural America—agriculture, equestrian sports and events, music, and entertainment. RFD-TV is available on cable, DIRECTV, and DISH network. Well-known trainers Clinton Anderson, John Lyons, and Craig Cameron are featured on RFD-TV programs.

Take a test ride on any horse you consider purchasing to see if the horse does simple things such as flex to both sides.

tip 8. Buying guide for "previously owned" horses

These basic elements should be included in any horse you consider purchasing for reining.

- Cue the horse to walk around the arena. You want the horse to move out easily and maintain a relaxed body language. Breaking gait or resisting forward motion are not good traits.

- Stop the horse and sit quietly. He should not move until you cue him.

- Trot around the arena. Again, look for a horse with a willing attitude that picks up the trot within four strides. Let the horse continue around the arena.

- Stop. Sit quietly. Watch for the horse to pull on the bit—a sign of impatience.

- Next, ask for a lope in the right lead. A desirable characteristic is for the horse to pick up the correct lead and lope without trotting first or taking more than four strides before loping. Switch to the left lead and continue loping.

- Bring the horse back to a walk and cue him to flex to both sides.

- Ask the horse to back.

Consider these parts of a test. Don't buy a horse that doesn't pass the test.

Chapter 2

Geared Up

Working with proper gear—from the saddle to the snaffle—enables you to focus less on the tack and more on making the smooth moves in the arena, which is your ultimate goal.

The thin brow band on this headstall works well with the structure of the horse's head.

tip 9. Looking good

When you are considering the headstall you'll use during reining, let your horse's head be the deciding factor. Some horses are more visually pleasing in a split-ear headstall versus the more popular brow band headstall.

Horses with small heads look even smaller and sometimes not proportionate in a brow band. Remember that the strong horizontal line across the brow will make the head look chopped into two pieces. Brow bands can be beneficial for horses with larger heads, for they distract from a long face.

The split-ear headstall offers an open face for the horse, which can keep the head looking balanced in proportion to the rest of the body. Use the split-ear on a small-headed horse. It works well on any head type.

Use protective foot gear, such as the splint boots shown here, during practices and performances. (photo courtesy of AQHA)

tip 10. Keep your feet

Always use protective foot gear on your reining horse. Splint boots protect a horse from hurting himself and provide additional leg support when put on properly. Splints should have the same tension as a leg wrap. Loose splints can cause friction that creates a sore. If a splint is too tight, it might bow a tendon. Leg wraps are not encouraged for the average competitor. Wrapping effectively requires extreme talent to disburse uniform pressure on the leg while protecting tendons and ligaments and keeping dirt from getting under the wrap. For these reasons, splints are the preferred protective leg gear for most reiners.

For horses that clip a front foot with a back foot during a reining pattern, incorporate bell boots into your daily gearing up process. The bell boot will protect the front feet without interfering with any maneuvers. After a few runs with the bell boots, the horse will also realize that he's not able to hurt himself and will relax during each run.

This horse is wearing skid boots on the hind feet for protection during stops.

tip 11. Skidding to a stop

When you are stopping a horse on any type of surface, always use skid boots. Skid boots are worn on the back legs and protect the fetlock. The most common skid boots provide a neoprene cover and a dense layer of foam rubber, which will be next to the fetlock. One trick to help keep debris from getting trapped inside the skid boot is to leave the bottom strap loose enough for dirt to escape. Avoid sheepskin lining on skid boots. It can hold in debris, which can aggravate the horse's legs.

It is better to have these protective items in place and prevent an injury, as opposed to treating an injury and nursing a horse back to competitive health. Be prepared for each ride before each ride.

The leather curb strap tied into the ring at the bit generates good response from minimal pressure on this horse's mouth. (photo courtesy of AQHA)

tip 12. Curb appeal

Each horse will determine if you get better results from a curb strap or a curb chain during training. A curb chain should be used when you need to get a little more response from a horse, but it shouldn't be used if it causes the horse to fear the bit. This is a fine line of distinction and should be approached with caution. It is easy to teach fear and hard to teach trust.

The curb strap can be used on a horse that responds lightly to the bit and doesn't need much correction. Since the goal of reining is to show the horse using minimal cues, determine which route will allow you to guide the horse without pulling too much. Be prepared to change as the horse grows through training and experience.

Please note that for some associations (i.e., the NRHA) showing in a curb chain is not acceptable—which is another reason to read and reread association rules before competing in a show.

tip 13. A bit to think about

When it comes to starting your two-year-olds, try spending a good amount of time in a short-shank snaffle as well as a ring snaffle. Remember, if used correctly this bit is no harder than the ring. A bit that utilizes leverage and a curb strap is a piece of tack that all riders eventually end up using on all of their mounts.

So if you ride your colts early in a short-shank snaffle, even if it is only once a week, these early bridle lessons will pay off greatly in the end when it comes to creating a horse that is a pleasure to ride. Be patient in allowing the colt to adjust to the pressure of the chin strap. Many young horses will tell you right from the start what type of mouth they are going to have: soft or tough, nervous or quiet. Also, keep the nosebands off while in the shank snaffle. Like the rest of the horse's body, the jaw needs to develop muscles to keep it shut and carry the bit properly.

The other positive aspect of early bridle work is that if progress isn't being made, you can always go back to the ring snaffle with no worries of rushing the colt. Just the act of walking them around one-handed in a bridle at the end of a work session will initiate the idea of neck reining, relaxing in a bit, and other subtle cues that will put them miles ahead of the rest as three-year-olds.

tip 14. Saddle up for a good ride

Use a reining saddle to achieve your best possible go. These saddles are built up in the front for support and help you maintain proper position when you sit down deep in the saddle for stops. The design of the saddle helps you put pressure on the horse at the correct points to help, not hinder, the spectacular sliding stops and other moves of the sport. You'll notice that a reining saddle pushes your legs forward and allows your legs to act as natural shock absorbers during stops. The stirrups will be narrow and provide a lot of movement. A reining exhibitor needs to be able to control leg movement. The specially built saddle will smooth the progress of your riding and create an environment for your horse to perform to its highest potential.

Wearing a breast collar during your reining practices and competitions can help keep your saddle in the proper place.

tip 15. Breast collars on for safety

Reining is a sport that involves numerous fast moves and quick stops. A breast collar should be worn every time you practice to keep the saddle in the proper position on the horse's back. The benefits are two-fold: you will learn as a rider where your body should be to maintain the correct position and your horse will be able to complete moves without having your misplaced weight throw him off balance. Some of the pros choose not to show in breast collars, and their reasoning is varied—from binding the horse during fast moves to personal preference. However, novice riders should add a breast collar onto their tack room requirements until otherwise advised by a trainer.

The clothing selected here has a simple, western style, fits properly and is color coordinated with the horse and saddle blanket.

tip 16. **What to wear**

Reining is an event where personality can be revealed through clothing. Most exhibitors opt for coordinated tops, chaps, and boots over jeans. Sparkly tops and snazzy chaps are more common to reining exhibitors now than ever before. Be sure the clothing is in its best shape before the show. Also, pack a backup outfit in case of an emergency.

Take this opportunity to look at your horse's coat color and think about coordinating colors literally from head to tail. You can match your saddle pad and even leg protection to your outfit and let it complement you horse's coat.

Display your personality, whether it is part showgirl or conservative cowboy—but don't go overboard. If you distract the judges by your choice of attire, how can you expect them to see the fantabulous moves your horse can perform?

tip 17. Fancy footwork

Reining horses are shown in horseshoes called *sliders*. Various associations can have different standards, so check to see what is legal under each association you are involved in. Then, schedule an appointment with a farrier you trust, has good recommendations, or has worked with other reining horses. After a few months of working with your horse and becoming familiar with the hoof growth and wear the shoes experience, the farrier should be able to help you establish a feasible schedule to have your horse properly shod before shows.

Pay attention to how your horse responds to being shod. If he remains tender for days after a visit from the farrier, take that into consideration in your pre-show schedule. It is not uncommon for a horse to throw a shoe at the show or moments before a show. More often than not, the on-site farrier will be able to tend to your shoeing emergency with ease!

tip 18. Stop stepping on your chaps

Before you show, you may find yourself in a time crunch. To save time, you'll find it easier to put your chaps on and continue getting the horse ready. Since most chaps are made longer than needed to walk in, turn up the bottom of the chap about 8 inches to create a cuff. This keeps your chaps clean and allows you to walk freely before the show begins. Once you are ready to get on your horse, simply turn the chaps down and you are ready to ride.

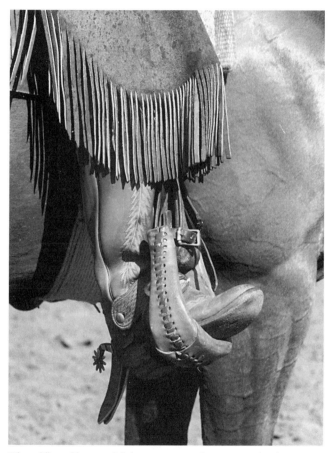

When riding with spurs, it is important to make contact only when you want to elicit a response. Here, the spur is kept away from the horse by keeping the heels down.

tip 19. Touchy subject

Spurs can be quite helpful or harmful when working with a horse. With a young reining horse, spurs should be used only when absolutely needed to elicit a response after all other cueing isn't working. Overusing the spur early in training will make the horse numb to it. Advanced horses may need a tap from a spur occasionally. During your rides, remain cognizant that you are wearing spurs. Keep your heels down and the spur away from the horse until you want to apply pressure.

When you purchase a horse, ask the owners about the horse's previous experience with spurs during the buying process.

Take time to examine your work environment to see if you need to make adjustments prior to beginning your reining practices.

tip 20. Working environments

While considering what elements you'll be executing with your reining horse, determine where you will practice these moves. Each facility will have different venues for circling, stopping, and riding your horse. Here are some things to consider.

- When you are working on large fast circles, you need room to ride the horse wide open. Some professionals have arenas as large as 150 feet by 300 feet to practice those large circles.

- A fence can be used to teach roll-backs and stops. Many facilities use a stopping track that consists of a stretch of dirt with a fragment of fence at the end. While this can be used, an arena with a fence can be utilized to teach more than just a stop and fulfill other training and riding needs

- Covered or indoor arenas are costly. However, whether it means building your own or joining a club that offers access, being able to supersede weather and daylight issues might make a covered arena worth the cost.

- Pipe is one of the best materials for fencing around horses. Wire can be dangerous. Weather can quickly have a negative impact on wood. However, pipe provides a relatively safe, smooth surface fencing material.

tip 21. Recycling can protect your pocketbook

Ladies, if you plan to enter numerous shows, you'll find that you either need numerous (read expensive) outfits or the names of one-hour dry cleaning services in all the cities you visit. Another option is to locate experienced show mavens who might be ready to part with the snazzy outfit they wore years ago. Weigh the pros and cons of recycling a sparkly vest or jazzy jacket. Many times, you'll be able to purchase previously owned attire at a bargain. Add the cost of any alterations that might be needed to make the clothing fit properly and you can still be below the price of a new outfit. Or, if you are handy with a sewing machine, consider creating your own designs.

tip 22. **Double-, no, triple-check equipment**

From latigos to stirrups, throat-latches to saddle pads, be sure to check your equipment before each ride. The quick-paced actions of reining mean that you can get into trouble even faster than you might during a recreational ride. Examine the leather on the saddle and headstall to make sure it is still usable. Check that saddle pads are clean and pliant so as to not rub sores on your horse. Validate that stirrups are attached correctly and will hold your weight. And don't forget to check splint boots and the like on your horse as well!

Bonus tip: After each use, maintain your equipment by cleaning, conditioning leather, and storing tack properly. This will extend the life of your equipment and improve your overall appearance at competitions.

Chapter 3

Elements of Training

A reining horse employs all of the basics of good horse training and some of the most intricate maneuvers one will ever ask of a horse. These elements are broken down and summed up in this chapter.

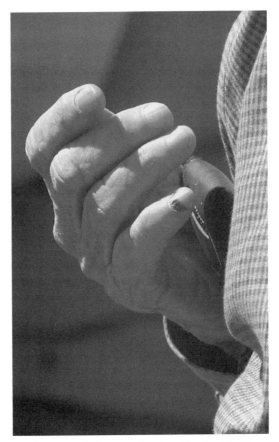

Hands can reveal a lot about the character of a rider. Even experienced riders can improve their riding by being aware of how they use their hands when cuing a horse.

tip 23. The genesis of soft hands

In the beginning, soft hands are not part of every rider's bag of tricks. Prepare for this human trait by using a forgiving bridle on your horse when you begin to learn the sport of reining. Something that is loose-jawed and won't aggravate the mouth is all you need. This allows you to use your instinct to gain your balance from the horse's mouth during a stop without deterring your horse's ability.

Then, you need to consciously try to be gentler with your hands and work toward upgrading your bit. This can be done by thinking of a small box placed over your saddle horn. Imagine that you have to keep your hands inside this 8-inch-square box and still accomplish all of the cues needed to get your horse to perform.

tip 24. What have you gotten yourself into?

Your reining horse will be expected to take on one of several reining patterns (ten, for instance, if you are competing in the National Reining Horse Association events). Luckily, most of the basics from show to show are the same—only the order and placement will change.

To complete the patterns presented in a reining class, you and your horse will need to have certain maneuvers in your repertoire. Before you begin training a new horse, realize that your goal is to be able to complete small slow circles, large fast circles, roll-backs over the hocks, flying lead changes, and complete 360-degree spins. These moves should only be part of what your well-broke horse can perform accurately to compete in the intense world of reining horses.

tip 25. Learning and age link

Reining horses have a lot to learn during training. Three-year-old horses that are guided down the futurity road are asked to learn and perform it all quite early on in life, while many of their peers are still running around the pasture. Take into consideration that these horses are basically adolescents. Be aware that showing a young horse can bring up many new areas for accident. Think ahead as to how the horse will react to the tractor plowing the arena before the show, the public announcement system, etc. Asking a well-broke horse to take these elements in is one thing; but a young horse might blow at something simple.

Pushing a young horse to grasp too many concepts can devastate the horse's mind. Don't compare your horse's progress to others. Keep the standard based on your horse's talent level and natural ability. Training is a slow process, so allow for gradual development. More often than not, you'll end up with a better horse than if you rush the job.

As part of her routine, exhibitor Kim Lindsey takes her horses straight from the arena to the pasture for riding in another environment.

tip 26. Get out and play

Take time to ride your horse outside of the arena. One of the most common mantras among top trainers is to get a horse outside to learn what kind of horse you have. Riding outside will show you the horse's temperament, athleticism, preferred rate of travel—and the list goes on and on. The goal is to ride without the distractions of other horses and riders, or the restrictions of fences you would find in an arena or round pen. During the first few rides, the aim is simply to spend time riding, which requires you to leave the horse's head alone.

A few trips out and you'll know more about how your horse travels (hopefully straight). It will take several rides for a young horse to become accustomed to carrying a rider any distance. During this time, his line will become straighter. Pick a spot a mile or so away and ride toward that spot using your legs to keep the horse headed straight. Using the reins to keep the horse on track can cause him to ignore the bit later in training.

Stalling a horse requires the rider to consider additional ways for the horse to exert energy.

tip 27. Are you stalled?

Some reiners find their horses have too much energy, and just riding them enough to work off that energy eats away at precious practice and training time. Many times, the riders aren't considering that stalled horses are limited in how they can exert energy. Stalled horses should be involved in some physical activity several times a day. Being turned out into an open pasture, placed on a mechanical walker, or led around will keep muscles toned, which prevents injury and soreness.

A career reining horse will benefit from the activity because they won't be as likely to become bored and develop vices that could hinder their performances.

This horse is flexing nicely at the poll in response to the light pressure the rider is applying to the reins. (photo courtesy of AQHA)

tip 28. Atta way to back into it!

Backing is another unnatural movement we ask horses to perform, but it is necessary to teach the horse about controlling the hindquarters. Before you attempt to teach a horse to back, the horse must willingly give his head in both directions. This lateral flexibility enables the horse to produce the movements that will make backing smooth and easy. Start while riding the horse around in a casual atmosphere. Stop the horse and gently ask him to back a few steps by picking up on both reins evenly to remove slack and then pull easily on one rein without moving the other. Do not apply constant pressure to the bit. That can cause the horse to jerk his head up when asked to back. Because you'll be causing him to move away from the bit, but in an unbalanced way, it will make him more likely to back up. Once you get the horse to respond by heading in the right direction, you can straighten out any crooked backing by applying equal pressure to the reins.

tip 29. Testing for lead change ability

One way to see if a horse is a natural at lead changes is to put him to the test. The test begins as you lope the horse in a large circle in the center of the arena. Do not let the horse drift toward the fence. After you've established the right lead, direct the horse toward the fence. The horse, faced with running into the fence, will shift his body weight. When you let him know from your leg and rein pressure which direction you expect him to head, he should change leads easily and continue at a lope in the correct lead down the fence.

tip 30. Loped and limbered

The start of any ride should consist of a warm-up. This helps prepare the horse and rider mentally. It also protects the horse physically by allowing muscles to become warm (hence the term *warm-up*) and flexible.

Begin by walking and trotting the horse in both directions, getting him to respond to the bit and leg pressure and, in general, becoming supple. But don't stop there. Before you begin going through any moves, lope your horse in big and small circles in both directions. Just as the jog isn't as intense as the run for you, the lope is a step up from the trot for the horse.

You want to get the horse supple in his legs, back, and shoulders. At the end of the warm-up, the horse should be relaxed, but not winded. It will take a few practice sessions to determine when you have the horse at the ideal state of warm-up. As the horse becomes more accustomed to the warm-up routine, you may need to adjust the time you warm up to fit his athletic ability.

Incorporating a new element to the horse's skill set, such as loping over a small jump, helps the horse stay attentive during each practice session.

tip 31. Go to Plan B

Include maneuvers other than the regular spinning, stopping, and lead changes that make up the reining performance pattern of a green rider's daily regime. This approach spices up the daily ride for both horse and rider. Some suggestions from Stephen Saidik of Cambridge, Ohio, are the counter-canter, side pass, and two-track. "Offering other exercises to work on besides the main points will help the horse and rider build communication in a way that working only on 'show' maneuvers could not," Saidik said.

Simple drills can keep the horse alert and help the duo avoid the frustration of a routine rut. During this early learning phase, the most important lesson for the rider is to figure out how the horse responds to "natural" aids of hands, seat, legs, and voice. Simultaneously, the horse will become acclimated to the rider's style and strength of cues.

Maneuvers can be picked up from other disciplines, such as barrel racing or Western horsemanship. The goal is to work different areas of the horse—hip, shoulder, neck, etc.—and create a supple movement in the horse with soft cues by the rider. When evaluating new moves, check that each one addresses movement and cues before incorporating it into a ride. After you've made it part of your practice sessions, re-examine the move to see if you can add onto the move to upgrade to the next level of skill.

For more seasoned horses, adding new challenges like a small jump can add much needed change to schooling sessions.

tip 32. Fence me in

Using the fence of a corral can help with many elements of training a reiner. Specifically, stopping can be improved by incorporating fence work in your daily routine. For a colt, trot alongside a fence, slow the horse, and pull him back toward the fence. Allow the rein that you are turning away from to have plenty of slack and pull on the rein you are turning into. The placement of the horse at the fence will cause him to rock his weight to his hindquarters. As the horse takes off in the other direction, he will drive with his hindquarters.

This accomplishes several things at once, which will become evident in the show ring. As you say "Whoa" while you are halting forward motion, the horse will begin to connect the command with the behavior. He'll begin to connect using the hock that is on the same side as the rein you are using to pull him around. Fence work encourages a horse to keep his back rounded and to turn on his hindquarters.

Practice this on both sides until the horse is able to turn back in either direction without losing impulsion. These tips can be used at a lope for a seasoned horse.

The verbal cue given by this rider helped the horse know when to execute this dirt-throwing stop. (photo courtesy of AQHA)

tip 33. Whoa equals stop

To teach the stop, start by trotting large circles. This middle gait allows the horse to have the impulsion needed to move his hocks under him during the stop and is easier to control than a lope. Trot several large circles and then proceed with the stopping cues. To ask a colt to stop, keep cues consistent and realize that the cues will be different from asking a seasoned horse to stop. Use a verbal cue (most often, you will say "Whoa"), sit down in the saddle, and then lightly pick up the reins. This sequence will allow the colt to begin to stop before you take control of his head. When the stop is complete, release the pressure on the reins, reinforcing that a correct action will result in release of pressure.

This is a good example of a hollowed-out back causing the horse to keep the legs straight during a stop. With more roundness in the back, the horse could free up his front end during the stop. (photo courtesy of AQHA)

tip 34. Stopping a young horse

With a young horse, it is best to keep the horse flexible in his front end by lightly pulling on the reins with slightly varied pressure. If you jerk the reins hard, you'll teach him to stiffen up his front end and jam his front feet into the ground. This results from having a scooped-out back. Remember, for a horse to stop using his back end, he needs to have a nice, rounded back. When performed correctly, the horse stops on his hind end with his hocks under his body, his back rounded, and his front feet free enough to "paddle" to a stop.

This photo is a good example of a horse stopping with a well-rounded back and using the feet to paddle to a stop. The exhibitor is centered, balanced, and staying out of the horse's mouth.

tip 35. Turn it into a stop

The fence work that helped your horse to use his hindquarters can be turned into the beginnings of a stop. After you've caused the horse to anticipate turning back into the fence, fake him out. For example, heading right in a trot or lope, determined by your horse's training level, your horse should expect to turn left into the fence. This is when you should ask him to turn right. Since he'll have been preparing to turn left, his left hock should be lined up underneath him. When you ask for the right turn, he'll put the right hock under him. This is a decent start for a stop since he'll be stopping forward motion, his back should be rounded, and he'll have his hocks under him.

Soon, you'll be on your way to having stops like the one exhibitor Steve Metcalf produced in this photo.

tip 36. Stirrup length can create a good stop

To put all of the pieces of the stopping puzzle together, take a look at yourself in the saddle. Stand up in your stirrups, being sure to straighten your legs. The pros tell us that you need to have at least 2 inches of daylight between your crotch and the saddle. Adjust your stirrup length until these measurements are correct. Short stirrups will make it harder than necessary to straighten your legs when you stop. Long stirrups can leave you reaching too much in an attempt to apply pressure to signal the stop to your horse. Incorporate the checking of your stirrup length into your practice routine as leather can stretch and you might need to readjust.

tip 37. Standing on solid ground

Arena conditions play an enormous role in your reining routine. Practice in ground that has been plowed, leveled, and plowed again. This will mimic the show conditions you will find at most shows. Not only will soft, loose, dry (but not dry enough to create dust) dirt make your practiced moves prettier, such dirt will also help keep your steed sound. Generally, if the ground is too deep, you run the risk of injuring tendons. If it is too hard, you are risking the hocks and stifles.

Although each horse person might have a different opinion on the "perfect" dirt, a good rule of thumb is for the dirt to almost reach the hairline above the hoof when the horse is standing still. Avoid running your horse on wet dirt, which has a tendency to bog around the feet and form hard clumps. To achieve the desired base, level the ground in your arena, apply water, pack the dirt, and then cover your base. Using a mixture of sand and dirt often makes for the best working ground. Be sure to keep dirt free from debris such as rocks, sticks, and other possibly damaging items.

tip 38. Maintain your foundation

The biggest mistake you can make after the ground is in place is not maintaining the surface. Personal preference and expense will determine if you use a sprinkler system or water truck. Both have benefits, but many of the larger horse operations select the water truck due to the control that watering system provides.

Most climates will require you to water the soil. The goal is to keep the ground moist enough to eliminate dust. However, water should never penetrate the ground to the extent that the base becomes wet. In an arid climate you will need to water more frequently to keep the dust at bay. In a humid climate you may find that watering twice a month with plowing in between waterings creates favorable conditions. Check out options in your area and examine a cost/benefit analysis before making any purchases.

tip 39. Are you strong enough?

Daily riding might not be enough to prepare your leg and back muscles for the strain of several sliding stops during a reining pattern. If you find that your trainer gets better results from your horse than you, it might be worth it to hit the gym and tone up those thighs before your next show. Horseback riding can be complemented by running or training on an elliptical machine. The goal is to increase strength, stamina, and flexibility—not to become overly muscled or be able to squat more weight than the guy next to you! Also, keeping the back muscles toned will help protect your spine if you do happen to execute a jarring stop. Check with a local gym to target these areas before you hit the show ring.

This exhibitor is riding the stop well. His legs are placed correctly and his body is controlled, allowing the horse to remain balanced. (photo courtesy of AQHA)

tip 40. Slowly we begin

Teaching the horse to stop is only part of the process. You also need to be able to *ride the stop.* Riding the stop can be taught through slow repetition. Start by walking the horse, saying "Whoa," stopping, and backing. This will let you experience the feel of stopping. From the walk, you'll learn how to position your legs and keep your center balanced during a full-on stop. Work up to completing the stop from a trot and, finally, a lope. During this slow-beginning process, you'll be learning to stop *with* the horse and follow him to the ground. You never want to try to force the horse to stop. It won't be long until you are ready to show off this stop in the show ring!

Notice how the rider is lined up perfectly with the center of the horse. (photo courtesy of AQHA)

tip 41. Stay centered

From the rider's perspective, achieving your best stop possible requires you to stay centered in the saddle. If your weight is not balanced, you can throw off your horse's ability to remain balanced. As you apply pressure through your legs into your stirrups and use your weight to sit down in the saddle, be aware of your center. Most people have a stronger side. Often, that correlates to the hand you write with (right-handed, stronger right side). To keep from throwing your horse off center, keep your head up and look ahead. When you look down, you are basically adding an off-center weight to your horse and asking him to balance it.

This horse is loping a circle with a natural head carriage. The neck is relaxed. The head is tipped slightly to the inside of the circle. (photo courtesy of AQHA)

tip 42. Get your head on straight

A comfortable performing horse is able to demonstrate a natural head position. Horses that twitch their tails during a performance or otherwise act irritated could be acting out because of a forced head carriage that throws off their balance. When a horse is relaxed, the head is naturally carried level with the withers. A tense horse usually keeps the neck high and rigid.

To get your horse to find his natural head carriage, you must ride him. Ride in a headstall and bit that the horse carries without fretting. Ride in a casual environment and check frequently to see that your horse is showing signs of being content. For example, the horse has his ears up, his eyes looking ahead, and he isn't reacting to your cues in a negative manner. When you reach this point, your horse is relaxed and his head carriage will be correct.

tip 43. Don't fall prey to fads

Remember this when you see a horse with an unusual head carriage winning at events: do not attempt to make your horse mimic this head carriage. It could be detrimental to the training progress you have made. A horse's head carriage is similar to how a human walks. We each have a distinct way of walking, but we still get around. Horses are the same way. If the head is too low, it can impede with getting the shoulders lifted enough to create impulsion. Too high, and the horse will not relax his front end enough to extend his legs forward. Consider that the winning horse may naturally have an unusual head carriage and yet perform all of the required moves exquisitely, leading to the win circle. Then, get back home and fine-tune your moves—not your horse's head carriage!

tip 44. Use your facilities to teach

Are you having trouble with your horse anticipating the flying lead change or just not hitting it in the desired, correct spot? Try these tips that incorporate the use of an arena fence.

First, make sure the horse is traveling correctly. If the horse is leaning out because he anticipates the lead change, the move can't be fixed until he's traveling in a balanced manner.

Once that is corrected, take off in a circle. When you arrive at the center of the arena, ask for the lead change but do not change direction; continue straight ahead. As you head toward the fence, bring the horse to a stop, but let the fence—not pressure from you—be the reason the horse stops. This teaches the horse to maintain a speed after the lead change. It also reinforces that a lead change doesn't always mean a change of direction.

Bonus tip: Reining phenomenon Dell Hendricks has a wonderful concept to mentally accept a lead change that doesn't work the first time. "Think of it as a busy signal. If you dial a number and it's busy, you don't jerk the phone off the wall and throw it down and stomp on it, you just dial again. With the horse, you just ask again. If he doesn't change leads the first time, stop and begin the whole process again."

tip 45. Graduation day

Give your young horse time to graduate from the basics of giving his head and controlling his limbs to the more detailed work of roll-backs and neck reining. Think of the training process as the graduation from elementary school to junior high to high school. If the animal doesn't have a foundation established during the first part of his education, he won't be capable of graduating to the next level. It is no different then students learning addition before they can move to long division—and we haven't even broached algebra yet! Don't rush graduation day or the holes in the education will come back to haunt you down the road.

tip 46. Keeping everything even

Most horses, like humans, rely and respond better with one side of their body. But with the work we're asking a horse to do during reining events, the horse needs to be ambidextrous or even-sided. A horse must respond evenly to light cues from the bit, reins, and rider's legs to be considered an even-sided horse. To check if your horse is responsive to the bit, make him flex at the poll and bend his neck toward your boot on both sides. Use a light pull on the bit and release pressure as soon as he responds by giving you his head. Making a circle in each direction while having the horse in a counter-arc will let you measure response to the rein. The counter-arc basically switches the body functions from a normal arc. In the counter-arc the horse's shoulder bends to the inside of the circle, the hip to the outside. Finally, the two-track is a good test for your horse's even reaction to leg cues. After you have determined which side of your horse needs work, you must work more often on the resistant side of the horse to create an equal response to cues.

tip 47. Go a half-turn first

As the old adage goes, you must learn to crawl before you can walk. The same is true in spinning. Before you accomplish the show-ready fast and flat spin, you must begin by doing a half-turn correctly. Start by backing the horse quickly. Release pressure from the right rein but maintain pressure on the neck with the left rein. The horse should move his head to the left.

Remember, the horse was moving backward when the pressure was released. So, he should move to the right, but also move up over the hocks. Keep your outside leg on him to keep momentum until the half-turn is complete.

This spin shows a nice example of the rider pushing the horse with leg pressure on the left and lifting the right leg off the horse. (photo courtesy of AQHA)

tip 48. A spinning top

Spinning shows control of the horse, because this isn't a move you'll see a horse perform on its own. Let's look at spinning to the right. The basic move is accomplished by laying the rein on the opposite side of the horse's neck. The horse should look to the right. From the horse's perspective, he knows that he needs to get away from the pressure that is being applied. Lift the reins slightly and your horse should respond by lifting the corresponding shoulder and beginning to arc the neck. Cue the horse with slight opposite leg pressure, sit back in the saddle, and the spin should begin. Do not rush this process. You are asking several responses at once and it could take time for the horse to process all the requests. Once the spin has begun and the horse is pivoting off his hind feet, maintain pressure on the opposite leg until you've completed as many rotations as the pattern requires, then release all pressure and the horse should come to a stop.

The proper use of leg pressure can make your days on horseback more enjoyable.

tip 49. Look at those legs

Leg control is a staple in the horse training laboratory. Trainers will tell you that teaching a horse to respond to leg pressure will make your days on horseback much more enjoyable. Leg control is used by picking up one rein and laying it against the horse's neck and simultaneously applying light leg pressure to that same side. A young horse may tend to turn his head into the rein that is being pulled. Keep the opposite rein just taut enough to keep the head straight. Remove any pressure from your opposite leg to give him room to go somewhere. Your goal? To get the horse to move away from the leg and rein that are pressing against him and continue forward motion. This loose translation of the two-track can be refined into a side pass when performed without forward motion. To teach this move, face the horse into a fence so that all movement is parallel to the fence.

As the rider practices a spin, the horse's body is following the nose. (photo courtesy of AQHA)

tip 50. Where the nose goes

Think of the spin. Have you ever thought of it from the horse's perspective? What looks so fluid from the stands is more complex for the performer. We're asking an 1,100-pound animal to move as quickly as possible around one foot. Not a normal move for a horse.

So, let's think about it like this: where you point that horse's nose, his body will follow. Basically, he's trying to catch his body up to his nose during the spin. To control speed, place the outside foot against the rib cage. A seasoned horse will naturally speed up in a spin to move away from that pressure. Release the pressure to stay at a certain speed, or to stop the spin.

Notice that the horse's hind end, back, and neck remain flat in the middle of this spin. This form is the most desired during a spin. (photo courtesy of AQHA)

tip 51. Fast and flat

To keep the spin fast and flat, you must have speed and form. The inside hind foot should be planted in the ground as the pivot point. The outside hind foot will be the instigator of motion, pushing off and helping to propel the body around. Helping the outside hind foot in creating motion is the outside front leg. The inside front leg serves as the balancing limb. It should touch down, balance, and then move over to keep the horse steady.

Experts in reining discourage using what are known as *loping turns* for your spins because the speed involved in the lope will cause the horse's front end to bob up and down, which defeats the form issue. The motion also slows the spin down and wastes time and energy bobbing up and down, rather than spinning in a flat formation.

A small pause between moves allows your horse to digest the lesson. Be it at practice, or during a competition, a brief pause is often quite beneficial.

tip 52. Rest and relaxation

Remember to give your horse time to allow lessons to sink in. When you've just executed a fantastic spin or stunning stop during a training or practice session, take the time to stop all movement. Let the horse stand and relax. Give some slack to the reins, relax your legs and seat, and sit patiently. Let the horse breathe a little, but not anticipate moving away from that spot. This simple action permits the lesson learned, be it big or small, to sink in. Perhaps this was one of the first times he didn't step on his own feet during the spin—and that lesson will be instilled and can be called upon the next time you attempt the spin.

Here a circle is being performed as the horse remains directly between the reins and moves quickly around the arena. (photo courtesy of AQHA)

tip 53. Round and round and round

In reining, the circle is the basis for everything. So performing a perfect circle will show a mastery of the event. The aim is for the horse to remain directly between the rider's reins while completing a circle. Being between the reins shows that the horse is under the rider's complete control. If your horse is leaning on a rein during the circle, he isn't responding to the cues that are needed to be a willingly guided mount.

To get the horse to the level of training where he'll stay between the reins, you can start by creating a foundation of neck reining.

This photo is a good example of a neck rein being applied to the right side and the horse moving to the left. (photo courtesy of AQHA)

tip 54. Neck reining

Neck reining, where a horse turns away from the weight of the rein on his neck, is the best way to start a horse in preparation for circles. If you begin the horse with the traditional training of responding to the direction the rein is pulled and then ask that horse to neck rein, expect some transition time between the two styles. Horses naturally move into pressure, whether it be neck or leg pressure. It will take time and effort to teach any horse to move away from pressure. Be patient and persistent. As soon as the horse moves away from the neck rein, release the pressure.

This palomino is hunting the circle. Notice that the rider sits confidently and is giving the horse its head as they go around the circle. That exhibits faith that the horse knows its job.

tip 55. Hunt your circles

Start by walking, trotting, or loping your horse in a circle and giving him his head, allowing slack in the reins. At this point, most horses will leave the circle. Teaching him to find the circle can be done by actually letting the horse leave the circle, then guiding him back to the middle of the circle. Then, allow him to work his way out to the same path you were on before and stay on that path. This teaches him that the path is not the important part of the circle: the center point of the circle is the focus.

Soon, the horse will be using the center of the circle as his focus. This is what reiners mean when they say they have a horse that *hunts the circle.* That horse is mindful of the center of the circle and goes around it with precision.

Repeat the process of giving him his head and seeing if he leaves the circle. If he leaves again, simply steer him back to the center of the circle and begin again.

tip 56. Manipulate mistakes into learning lessons

Whether it is leaving the circle or spinning more times than he should, if you can stay out of your horse's way by limiting pilot errors, your horse will learn from his own mistakes. Allow a mistake, then correct it. Allow the horse to err again, correct again and continue. Sooner or later, he'll connect leaving the circle with starting over and will realize that staying between the reins (and in the circle) results in less work from him. Even animals that "love their jobs" can respect putting in an honest day's work and getting a break.

tip 57. A straight circle

When performing a circle, the horse's body should be, oddly enough, straight. The head is the only part of the body that should exhibit any curve, allowing you to see part of the inside eye. That glimpse of the eye is enough to tell you that the horse is moving correctly. A horse will look where he's headed; if he straightens his head, you'll soon notice that you are nearing a fence. To reinforce the idea of looking where you are going, think about steering your horse like you would a car. The body of your car doesn't bend; the wheels and workings in the under-carriage do. Think of the horse's body from the withers back as the car body—a straight line that must remain that way to stay balanced.

You might be forcing the horse to lean on the inside rein if you are trying to hold the horse's shoulders up to keep him between the reins. To teach the horse to circle on his own, you'll find that natural balance occurs when the horse is keeping his head slightly tilted to the inside of the circle. When you relax your inside leg and rein pressure, the horse may leave the circle. If so, guide him back to the center without pulling on his mouth and he'll learn to move symmetrically around the center point of the circle, after time and repetition.

Flying lead changes are difficult to photograph. Here you see the horse has shifted the weight from the right side to the left side as they begin the circle to the left. (photo courtesy of AQHA)

tip 58. Flying into your lead changes

Flying lead changes are a daunting task for a rider. To change from one lead to another, the horse needs to make a forward-moving lead change. Often, the rider is thinking of a lateral change from right to left, or vice versa. Instead, consider it as a continued movement forward, changing only which foot comes first. Many riders try to shove the horse into changing leads with their weight. This will disrupt forward motion and cause the horse to respond too much to the shift of balance.

Using leg pressure and neck rein pressure should be enough to generate the lead change. Mentally, you should think of asking for the lead change rather than forcing the lead change. Don't expect the flying lead change to happen immediately. Lope circles at a steady pace to the right and then, ask for a lead change as you change directions. Mark in your mind where you want the lead change to occur in the arena. Set up your horse to hit that mark and gently guide him to that spot. Ask for the change with leg pressure (usually applying leg pressure on the opposite side of the requested lead) and gentle neck rein pressure. If you request the change by applying too much pressure, it will be easily detectable to a judge. Have you seen a horse kick out during a lead change? That's the horse's show of frustration, on display for the whole world to see. That is not what you want. After several practices, you'll fall into the proper rhythm of when and where you should prep the horse for the change to get it to happen at the center of the arena and the top of the circle.

If problems occur, try recording your practice runs. Reviewing the actual act can make it easier to see where you might be getting in your horse's way or where your horse might be ignoring your cues, and why.

tip 59. I bought a broken horse!

Buying a horse trained by an unknown person can create some interesting learning curves for the new rider. As you are discovering the idiosyncrasies of your horse, remember that training styles can differ from barn to barn, much less region to region. You may find that your horse simply will not try to get away from leg or rein pressure. Consider that he might have been trained to counter-arc to pressure.

There isn't a good, better, or best way to train a horse, as long as you know what you will get in answer to applying leg and neck rein pressure. In this case, remember that you'll be using your leg and rein pressure to lead the horse rather than push the horse away.

tip 60. Dropping to the trot

When working on lead changes, avoid dropping gaits to the trot to allow the horse to pick up the correct lead. Permitting the horse to perform a lead change at a trot and then speed back up to the lope will only create acceptance for the lazy lead change in the horse's mind. Plus, once you've allowed the horse to cheat on a lead change during practice, it won't be long until that training lapse is visible to all in the show ring. Maintain your training and practice to its highest level and your shows will be of the same caliber, if not better.

tip 61. Size really doesn't matter

Circles are an important element to any reining pattern, and almost everyone has a different opinion on how to ride the perfect circle. But one thing most seem to agree on is that the shape of the circle is more important than the size of the circle.

Check out the area you are riding in and balance your circles to that space. This will be beneficial when you train or compete in various arena sizes. If your horse leaves the route of the circle you want to ride, gently correct him until he's back on the right path. Your job is to keep the shape of the circle balanced and, obviously, circular.

tip 62. Keeping it fresh, moving fast

During training and practices, you have the option of pounding one maneuver into your horse's head until he gets it or keeping things fresh. The experts that win in this class will tell you that they have the best response when they move quickly between moves—be it during training, or in practice before a show. If you note the smallest step forward in a horse's training on one move, reinforce the learning by moving on to another element. Keeping the sessions interesting for the horse will keep the successful rides to a maximum for you.

tip 63. A seasoned, yet crooked horse

Some advanced horses back up crooked. Sure, it would have been nice to work that kink out during the colt years, but it's a fact of life. To remedy the problem, use leg pressure to keep the horse in the proper alignment. Do not try to correct the horse with the reins, as you can cause him to become dull in the mouth. If the horse is drifting to the right, use your right leg to bump the horse back to a straight position, and vice versa. Remember that the goal of backing, either in the show ring or at home during practice, is to get a horse to back easily and willingly. A horse that can back a straight line with minimal correction, well, that's just a bonus!

Riding alone can help you learn how your horse will handle the show ring. Take time to incorporate being the only horse in the arena to your practices. (photo courtesy of AQHA)

tip 64. Ride alone

One way to prepare your horse for the day of competition is to get him comfortable with being in the arena alone. Horses are herd animals and instinct tells them that safety is in numbers. This isn't a problem if you normally ride alone. However, if you are constantly with another horse in the arena, ask the other riders to leave the arena for a few minutes. Set up your horse and see how he responds to being alone. Your goal is to have a relaxed horse. If he doesn't seem as relaxed as you want, devote more time to riding alone in the arena before you take him to a show.

This rider selected a schooling show to get an official critique on her performance and expose her horse to the show scene.

tip 65. Back to school for you

A novice rider should take advantage of any schooling shows in their area. Schooling shows provide the fast-paced atmosphere and time schedule of an actual show without the hefty entry fees or soaring stress levels. These shows provide a great training ground for younger horses, as they allow them to experience everything from unfamiliar horses in their territory to the sounds of the public announcement system. For seasoned performers, schooling shows provide a place to maintain performance levels and work out small kinks between shows. They also allow you to get your routine down for warm-ups before a show. Check into the schooling shows around your area to find those that work best for you.

tip 66. Gimme a break

When you hit a bump in the training road and can't seem to get past it, take a break. There is no golden rule that says if you don't ride every day, you are bound to fail. Give yourself time to contemplate what you are doing during each training session and allow those developments to come to fruition at a natural pace. Use the days you take a break from riding to check on your equipment, clean out your tack room, watch videos of new training options, or enjoy your favorite hobby outside the horse world.

tip 67. Stubborn ol' cuss

Do you have a stubborn backer on your hands? If the horse doesn't give his head or has been mishandled by another rider and has become protective of his tender mouth, try this method. Find a bit to soften his mouth. Then tie each rein to the D-rings on each side of the saddle. You want the reins to be (a) even, (b) tied securely, and (c) adjusted so that moving his head into the vertical will alleviate the pressure from the bit. Turn him loose in an arena or round pen that is free from any dangers while he is tied. Also, make sure you keep an eye on him during this process. It doesn't take long for the horse to learn that by tucking his nose and giving to the reins, he'll find relief— and that's a good first step in getting him to back without incident.

Chapter 4

Competition Day

It is what you've been preparing for— the day of competition. Use the tips here to help make that first day in the arena a positive experience for you and your horse.

tip 68. Keeping track of papers

Obtain a three-ring binder to keep all your necessary papers for the day of the show. This list can include association membership cards, horse's registration papers, medical information (i.e., Coggins papers), and any other paperwork related to your horse. Use plastic sheets to keep the papers protected. Then store the notebook in your vehicle or trailer as you go from show to show. As an added benefit, if you decide to sell or breed your horse, you'll know where to look to get the papers for the new owner or breeder.

tip 69. Preparedness plan

A few days before the show, prepare to be on the road. Clean out your truck and trailer, then load the grain, water, hay, tack, and other equipment you will need for the show. Check tire pressure and fill up the gas tank. Get driving directions and make sure you have the maps you might need.

This may seem routine, but if you can incorporate this element of work into your plan, it will make your showing experiences more consistent and become a source of contented busyness for you as the show approaches. Since you will be ahead of the game, in the sense of creating order from chaos, your mind can focus on the show and taking care of your horse.

A good rule of thumb for a novice warm-up is to have your trainer guide you from the sidelines.

tip 70. Novice warm-up

Do it yourself. If you are a novice rider, ask your trainer to give you guidance from the sidelines as you warm up the horse. It might seem easier to let the trainer get the horse ready, but this warm-up time is an invaluable opportunity to work out jitters and get in tune with your horse. Before you begin the warm-up, let the trainer know which areas you really need feedback. Plus, being able to do it yourself will make the run have more significance to your learning and progressing in the sport.

tip 71. Cinch up often

Oftentimes, multiple people assist with the horses on the day of the show. And multiple people have multiple ways of handling horses. When this is unavoidable, take precautions to keep yourself safe, such as double-checking that the cinch is tightened before you step into a stirrup. The last person to touch the saddle might have left the cinch loose to allow the horse to get more air after warm-up or when running a pattern at the show.

tip 72. No fighting allowed

The day of the show is not the time to fix a problem. Instigating a fight before a show is like picking on your spouse as you head to the family Christmas get-together: no good will come of it, and in the end, you'll probably have a horrible time as a reminder of the fight. If you haven't corrected the problem before you get to the show, reconcile the fact that your horse's ability level is what it is. Then show to the best of that ability. Stay calm, focused, and do your best. The upside is that there is still room for improvement!

Here exhibitor Bill Smith allows his horse to catch a breath between maneuvers.

tip 73. Air out

Remember to give your horse time to catch his breath during your warm-up on the day of the show. It is best to allow time for him to relax and breathe between each move you are practicing. During your warm-up, you'll want to run the horse as fast as you plan to run him during the show, following thirty to forty minutes of slow loping. You need the horse to exert all of his energy and suck air, so that you don't take him into the arena too fresh to respond to your cues. Figuring out the right amount of time to allow between running during the warm-up and showing will take practice. Allow at least forty-five minutes of getting their breath before you show. As you learn more about your horse, adjust accordingly.

With a well-planned strategy, you could soon find yourself performing with the smooth moves of this duo. (photo courtesy of AQHA)

tip 74. **Showtime**

On the day of the show, you'll perform better if you have a game plan. If you have certain people who help you stay focused, let them hang out with you before the show. Delegate duties—and you can make them feel involved while you reduce your own workload. Determine if you need a general to-do list or an hour-by-hour breakdown of your day's schedule. Then refer to this list. It will help keep you calm before entering the arena, which will help your horse relax before the big event as well.

Some competitors serve as their own competition. Make sure you aren't setting yourself up for a self-destruct by over-thinking and under-planning your game-day strategy.

This exhibitor shows confidence in his body language and the authority he has as he guides his horse. This level of showmanship ups the playing field for everyone. (photo courtesy of AQHA)

tip 75. Showmanship really shows

When it comes to separating the born competitors from the rest of the gang, confidence is everything. Ride with confidence and keep your head up, shoulders back, and heels down. Take control and make the judge sit up in her chair and take note. When judges are putting in twelve and fourteen hours per day, sometimes you have to get them to notice you with your confident look and abilities. It is easy to differentiate between the riders who are just going through the motions, and the ones who came ready to win.

tip 76. Know your surroundings

Take into consideration the climate where you are competing. Humid air, elevation, excessive heat, and other environmental elements can influence your horse's performance and recovery time. If possible, research the climate of the venue you'll be attending and attempt to mimic those conditions prior to leaving for the show. Another option is to arrive at the location a day or two early and practice with your horse. This helps to acclimate the animal and lets you know what to expect on competition day. To keep horses on track at out-of-town shows, some owners will haul water and hay to keep the horses eating and drinking as they would at home.

tip 77. Do not quit

Keep in mind that the judges will adjust the score of the run as it is happening, so start strong and finish strong. Never quit showing. No matter what happens in the pattern, keep your head up and finish the pattern as if you want to win. You never know how everyone else is going to do. And if you keep your mind on the task at hand and your attitude positive, you could have a positive outcome to a less-than-perfect run.

tip 78. Mental workout

Before you enter the show ring, mentally review your pattern for the day. Think about each circle, stop, pause, lead change, roll-back, and spin. Place the maneuvers where you want them to occur in the arena. Envision your lead changes in the middle of the arena and at the top of the circle.

This practice also allows you time to slowly evaluate what might have been less than perfect in your last practice or performance and to fix it mentally—which is a positive step toward fixing it in reality.

tip 79. Anticipate anticipation

Horses are intelligent animals. Intelligent enough that they can easily become burned out on the patterns we mere humans have them run during reining classes. The problem is that you need to practice the pattern but prevent the horse from practicing the pattern.

So, break the pattern up into pieces and practice a piece at a time during your warm-up the day of the show. Do not practice the pieces in order. Break them up and you'll keep your horse more alert to small cues during actual show scenarios. This is especially important with younger horses, to prevent anticipation of cues once you begin a run.

A professionally shaped hat is a sign of a serious competitor.

tip 80. To the top of the head

Invest the time and money to have your hat professionally shaped. This is the one pet peeve many judges have with exhibitors. Hats make a big impression. If you come in the arena and your hat looks like you have been out on the range rounding up cattle, or you slept in it last night, it will have an effect on your score. Your hat is the very first thing a judge sees. Make a good impression. Plus, once the hat passes inspection, the judges can focus more on what you and your horse do during the run.

This exhibitor is clearly looking at a spot over his horse's head while performing the stop. (photo courtesy of AQHA)

tip 81. Day-of-show stopping solutions

On the day of the show, you'll find yourself doing things you've never done during practice. And after you've almost blown the pattern, turned too many times, and cued too early on a lead change, you'll have one last chance to end on a positive note. To get the best stop out of your horse, never look at the place where you'd like the stop to occur. Keep your eyes set on the fence at the end of the arena, or even beyond that point. This will keep you relaxed and your body will stay in rhythm with the horse.

Backing up without pausing could cause this horse to step on its tail because of how close the hind end is to the ground.

tip 82. Tail troubles

A perfect run can be hindered right at the end with the simple backing move. Many horse and rider duos are docked on the score sheet when the horse trips over its own plentiful tail. How could this happen? Well, remember you'll cue your horse faster in the show ring than you've ever done before. But if you are aware of this show ring fact, you can counteract it. More often than not, the horse will be deep on his hocks after the final stop. If you will allow the horse to get his feet back under him before asking him to back, you can avoid losing those precious points. Patience equals points!

tip 83. Save your patterns

The show can be a great way to prepare for your next training endeavor. At each show you attend, save a copy of the patterns that are being run during the show and start a notebook of patterns, which you can use them from time to time when you are training. Referring to these patterns as guides can help you keep your practices varied. Incorporate easy and difficult patterns into your rides as a way to test yourself and your horse. Working through the patterns as you practice will also keep the elements in an unexpected order for your horse.

tip 84. All I know is that I know nothing

Use your time in the warm-up arena at shows to learn from other riders and trainers. Observe how horses respond to certain training methods. Examine riders to see what they are doing differently from you. Converse with successful trainers and exhibitors about their methods. Watch other competitors as much as time allows. Then watch your run on video, or get a critique from a trainer you admire, and compare your run to others. This will allow you to improve your own performance and help you get to know more about the industry.

Cooling down the sweaty horse is an important part of caring for a reining horse.

tip 85. Cool down

Make time after your run to cool your horse down. A few minutes of trotting and then walking in the warm-up arena will give your horse time for muscle recovery. You should walk the horse until he has stopped sweating and feels cool to the touch. Dependant on the weather, rinse sweat and dirt off the horse and you'll lower his body temperature. Using cool water will stimulate the horse's circulation and prevent soreness. Failing to cool down your horse properly can lead to a condition that affects the nervous system called *azoturia*, or tying-up.

tip 86. Treating an injury at the show

If the worst-case scenario of injury occurs at the show, think before you treat. Educate yourself on the medications approved for use by the associations you show with prior to administering any drugs. Working within the confines of the approved medication list will get you back on the show circuit as soon as possible when your horse recovers from the injury. Overreacting to an injury and treating with a medication that isn't legal can force you into downtime that will set you and your horse back. Taking things slowly can prevent you from making a medicating mistake.

tip 87. Coming back from injured reserve

Reining classes have grown in the past decade to facilitate horses that are six and older. This increased age span offers horses that have suffered an injury in their first years of showing to recover and hit the show circuit again. But how do you get your horse back in the arena without aggravating the injury?

Start slow. First you'll need to get the horse's muscles back in shape. So begin by walking the horse for five to ten minutes a day. This will build strength in a horse that hasn't been worked recently. Build up to walking and trotting for fifteen minutes each day. Allow the horse one day off a week. You should see marked improvement in the horse's muscle tone from the daily walking before you begin trotting. Incorporate long-trotting and an extra ten minutes to the daily schedule. Long-trotting loosens the horse up and is a good move to add to his routine before loping. Finally, when the horse shows to be sound and keeping his wind, try loping. On average, it will take a month of this type of work to prepare a horse to be ridden daily and prepped for a show.

Turning a horse out allows it to fall into the normalcy of being a horse, which is often needed if your show season is hectic.

tip 88. Are you riding too much?

A seasoned reining horse deserves some time off every now and then. One of the hardest things for a rider to know is when to quit. Seasoned horses know their jobs, but if you ride them too often or drill elements too hard, the horse can begin to hate his job. Evaluate your need to ride versus the damage riding too much could have on your horse. It is best to warm up, work on a few moves, cool the horse down, and put him away. Turn the horse out for a day or two when you have the opportunity. The fresh perspective that you will both have during your next ride will be beneficial.

After the show, reflect on what you've accomplished during that performance. (photo courtesy of AQHA)

tip 89. Use your resources

After the show, take the time to speak to a judge about your run, if possible. Look over the score sheet and determine if you were docked for a mistake you didn't realize you made. Politely approach the judge and ask concise questions to learn how to improve your run. Do not monopolize a judge's time, but make the best use of that availability. It is better to leave a show knowing exactly where you lost points and why you kept them, as opposed to showing, getting a score, and leaving—only to repeat the same mistakes at the next show.

tip 90. The nitty gritty

When you've determined that a horse has recovered from an injury by completing tip 87 you need to get to the nitty gritty of the reining foundation. Begin by making sure the horse is supple. This can be done by bending him at the hip and neck and moving him across the diagonal. Check that he is guiding correctly by trotting some slow circles. He should stay between the reins. If he's having problems, you can help him remember his training by trotting figure eights until he falls back into the habit. Then, lope circles in both directions, fast and slow. Loping circles is the final part of getting your horse loosened up.

Once you feel the horse is relaxed, incorporate lead changes, stops, or spins. Don't pressure him to be perfect; use this time as a measuring stick to tell you how much time he'll require before he's ready to show again. Once you've gone through the work you want to do for the day, walk around the arena a few times to cool him down and let him catch his breath.

tip 91. Let me change your mind

It is easy for competitors to lose sight of their exact goal when they get into competition mode. When you perform in a reining competition, you should determine if your goal is to have a certain score, execute a perfect move, or simply maintain the level of performance you've been able to show before. Perhaps none of these things will occur, but you still have to discover the positive aspects of your performance. Mind-set is an important aspect of reining. Creating an impossible dream for your horse is certain to result in failure. You'll find that it is easier to keep working toward your goals with a positive, realistic mind-set.

tip 92. The don't list

Everyone should have an idea of what they want to accomplish with their reining horse and what *not* to do.

- **Don't** let other people's scores change your attitude or warm-up the day of the show.

- **Don't** practice the pattern you'll be performing.

- **Don't** wait until the last possible moment to consider attire and tack.

- **Don't** forget to thank those who helped you at each show.

- **Don't** out-think yourself. Prepare mentally to stay on top of the game.

- **Don't** put too much importance on draw order. First or last or somewhere in the middle, your run and not your order should make you stand out to the judges.

- **Don't** forget that forcing yourself or your horse to compete too soon can ruin the show for you both. Take your time!

Chapter 5

Continuing Your Reining Education

The fool is one who fails to continue learning. After you have fallen in love with competing in reining classes, it is always good to keep learning. These tips will help you add to your bag of tricks in the sport of reining and beyond.

tip 93. Review the rules

As you progress from a beginner to an expert, be sure you stay current with the rules and regulations of your associations. Rulebooks are amended and standards can change. It is better to stay on top of that information than be surprised by something new at a show. Becoming involved in the association as much as possible will allow you to keep your finger on the pulse of the sport. Keep up to date on judging standards as they can change through the years. This is especially important if you take a few years off of showing and then resume your reining endeavors.

tip 94. Scholastic endeavors that begin horseback

Research the possibilities of putting your horse into the college fund for your child. How? If your child competes well in reining, many collegiate equestrian teams might come to the table with a scholarship. Equestrian teams often need riders with experience handling and riding top-notch horses. If your youth is showing, don't let this financial opportunity slip away. Look into options with the National Reining Horse Youth Association, AQHA, Intercollegiate Horse Show Association, and the United States Equestrian Federation. Most groups require membership to be eligible, but that's a small price to pay for the possible return.

tip 95. Not your average horse sale

Each year, you have the opportunity to purchase horses from a select group of reining horses at four sales sponsored by the NRHA. The sales include everything from broodmares and stallions to yearlings and two-year-old prospects. Under the management of the NRHA, the sales provide horses from world-renown trainers and breeders in the reining industry. And, not just any old horse hits the sale ring. Horses are accepted for consignment based on pedigree, produce records, and a visual inspection. Check out the sales in Oklahoma City during the NRHA Futurity in December and NRHA Derby in May.

tip 96. Become an apprentice

The NRHA offers an apprenticeship program where nonprofessionals can train under a member of the NRHA Professionals. This allows you to show as an Open rider without the restrictions of sitting out three to five years if you sign your Open card and then decide not to become a professional. The twelve-month program will allow you to compete on a whole new level and see if you are ready to take the step toward becoming a professional trainer in the reining industry. However, once you've become an apprentice, you cannot show as a non-pro for that year.

Apprentices have two options after the year-long program: remain an Open rider, thus relinquishing the NRHA Non-Pro classification, or return to non-pro status without the normal wait to reapply for non-pro status.

tip 97. Off the growth chart

Tried-and-true reiners are horse people who love the challenge of making an 1,100-pound horse move as gracefully as an ice-skater. And these same people like to keep the excitement coming. So, once you've tackled your first reining goal, stay alert to where you want to go next. It might be a new horse, a new level of competition, a new classification of event, or even taking a leadership role in one of the many reining-related associations. Look ahead in the requirements and restrictions set in place by such groups as far as winnings, so that you can take full advantage of the options reining offers. As reining is on the verge of becoming an Olympic event, the possibilities are seemingly endless!

tip 98. Giving to a good cause

Check with your local 4-H groups and other horse-related groups to see if you can lend a hand by judging local competitions after you've become a successful reiner. You'll be able to use your reining knowledge to encourage another generation of reining horse enthusiasts while you remind yourself of the basics of the sport. Taking a look at what the youth are accomplishing might revamp your approach. It may also provide an opportunity to scout out some quality trainers or horses. Every opportunity should be seized!

Freestyle reining allows the rider creative freedom including outfits for the horse and rider that carry out the theme of the routine. (photo courtesy of AQHA)

tip 99. Be a freebird

At some point, the standard routines might become too mundane for those creative souls out there. To remedy your need to be creative, check out the opportunity to enter a freestyle reining event. Not only are these competitions tons of fun for the fans, the exhibitors love them as well. Most freestyle shows allow exhibitors to develop their own pattern, set to music and with costumes to help depict the characters.

Many reining horses are also good reining cow horses, as is the case with AQHA stallion Real Gun, ridden by Chris Littlefield.

tip 100. Add a cow

After a few years of showing in reining classes, you might want to jazz things up a bit. A natural progression for many reiners is into the reined cow horse classes, like those offered through the National Reined Cow Horse Association (www.nrcha.com) or the American Quarter Horse Association (www.aqha.com). The horse should have all the required reining knowledge to ace the reining portion of the classes. The introduction of a cow into the daily practice schedule will give you plenty of new kinks to work out as a team.

tip 101. Reining is not for beginners

Reining is a flourishing equestrian sport, and it seems to be on its way to becoming an Olympic event. However, reining is not for beginning riders.

The complicated moves are made to look seamless and flowing because of hard work and eons of practice time. If you are a beginning rider and new to horses, work toward the goal of showing in reining but don't make the mistake of expecting it to be your first event on week three of riding.

Instead, make reining a goal on your horsemanship to-do list. Understand that the maneuvers used in reining can crossover to help you in other classes (i.e. Western horsemanship) that will help you establish a foundation of showing and riding on your horse before you attempt a reining class.

Additional Reining Information

The National Reining Horse Association
3000 NW 10th St
Oklahoma City, OK 73107-5302
405.946.7400
www.NRHA.com

The American Quarter Horse Association
P.O. Box 200
Amarillo, TX 79168
Customer Service: 806.376.4811
www.AQHA.com

The American Paint Horse Association
P.O. Box 961023
Fort Worth, TX   76161-0023
Office: 817.834.APHA (2742)
Fax: 817.834.3152
www.apha.com

National Morgan Reining Horse Association
R2 883 Tipperary Road
Oregon, WI 53575
608.835.7442
www.nmrha.com

Appaloosa Reining Horse Association
8590 W 12th Street Road
Juniata, NE 68955
402.751.2252
www.aprha.com

Arabian Reining Horse Association
Eleanor Hamilton, President
Phone: 763.786.8750
Fax: 763.786.6543
www.arha.net

Locate Professional Horse Trainers
www.4ahorse.aqha.com

Watch Reining Horse Trainers on Television
www.rfdtv.com

Noted Reining Horse Trainers

Stephen T. Siadik, reining trainer and exhibitor
Cambridge, Ohio
Phone: 740.432.4373
Email: stsph@aol.com
www.stsperformancehorses.com

Hendricks Reining Horses, Inc.
14974 E. FM 922
Tioga, TX 76271
Barn: 940.437.5157
Dell's cell: 940.372.0259
www.hendricksreininghorses.com

Tom McCutcheon Reining Horses, Inc.
3982 Warschun Rd.
Aubrey, TX 76227
Barn: 940.381.0880
Tom's Cell: 940.390.RIDE (7433)
www.tmccutcheon.com

Schmersal Reining Horses, LLC
Craig Schmersal
P.O. Box 130
Overbrook, OK 73453
Office: 580.224.2679
Craig's cell: 580.222.9565
www.scmersalranch.com

Craig Johnson Reining
3725 FM 2071
Gainesville, TX 76240
Phone: 940.665.6230
Fax: 940.665.7642
www.craigjohnsonreining.com

Books

Reining: The Guide for Training & Showing Winning Reining Horses, by Al Dunning and Pat Close

If I Were to Train a Horse, by Jack Brainard

Reining: The Art of Performance in Horses, by Bob Loomis

Training the Reined Horse, by Peter Phinny and Jack Brainard

International Reining Associations

Austrian Reining Horse Association
A-2563 Pottenstein
Kremesberg 15 Austria
001-43-2238-8484

Belgium Reining Horse Association
Engelselei 84
2140 Borgerhout Belgium

British Columbia Reining Horse Association
Box 702
Armstrong BC Canada V0E 1B0
250-546-8998

Central Germany Reining Horse Association
Fahrenbacher Str. 119
Fahrenbach, Germany 64658
49-6253-7470

German Reining Horse Association
Amtsgarten 1
D-63916 Amorbach
West Germany

Italian Reining Horse Association
Via Repubblica, 6
43056 Gainago Di Torrile
Parma, Italy
0521-819151

Japan Reining Horse Association
556-17 Terasaka
Oiso-machi
Nakaguun, Kanagawa Japan 259
81-463-72-1910

Reining Horse Association of Holland
Oranjewoudstraat 18
2552 RL Den Haag
Netherlands
011-31-70-3659542

Scottish Reining Horse Association
Elmwood House
Campmuir, Coupar Angus
Perthshire, PH13 9LN
01828670624

Steigerwald Reining Horse Association
Zum Lockfeld 10
D-66399 Mandelbachtal, Germany
011-49-6803-1844

Switzerland Reining Horse Association
Riedstr. 224
Aeugstertal, Switzerland
01-760-00-61